Brunch
with
Steffi

Elizabeth Grey

ISBN: 978-1-7366833-3-0 (print)

ISBN : 978-1-7366833-4-7 (e book)

Because of the dynamic nature of the internet, any web addresses or links contained in this book may have changed since publication and may no longer be valid. The views expressed in this work are solely those of the author and do not necessarily reflect the views of the publisher, and the publisher hereby disclaims any responsibility for them.

Publisher:

Tressie's Tales

PO Box 388

Libby, MT 59923

Editor: Melinda Gholson

This book is a work of non-fiction. Unless otherwise noted, the author and the publisher make no explicit guarantees as to the accuracy of the information contained in this book and in some cases, names of people and places have been altered to protect privacy.

4

DEDICATION

This book is dedicated to the memory of Stefania Petruch Carlson, a survivor of World War II Concentration camps. She was a loving wife, mother, grandmother, and great-grandmother.

     Pictures of tea cups have been placed throughout this book as a symbol of my brunch with Steffi because these teacups belonged to Steffi. She had a collection of some very unique designs.

TABLE OF CONTENTS

ACKNOWLEDGEMENTS

The first person I would like to thank is my husband, Randy Carlson, for his encouragement on this project. His personal interest in the story is expected because it is about his mother. But, because he and his siblings knew very little about her life before she married their father, he was excited anytime I was able to discover additional facts.

After Steffi's death in 2014, Caran Carlson LaBarge, Randy's sister, found documents and pictures in their mother's belongings which provided a record of portions of her pathway from Germany to America.

Joylynn Carlson, Randy's cousin, was again supportive of this book as she was with my first attempt at writing. Special thanks to her for writing the Foreword in this book.

Another important participant in this undertaking was Johanna Feret. She so graciously interpreted the letter we found from a family member in Poland addressed to Steffi. Johanna is an immigrant from Poland who has been in the United States since she was young child. She has continued to speak her native language and was extremely helpful with both the content of the letter as well as the general meaning/intent of the comments.

Once again, I must thank my cousin, Melinda Roseberry Gholson, for editing this book. It is a very time consuming and tedious task!

FOREWORD

Sometimes history is something we learn in a big book when we are in school. Sometimes history is happening all around us as we live daily life. I have been reminded in recent days, history is constantly written. The people memorialized in "Brunch with Steffi", were part of my everyday life. Elizabeth joined our family when she married Randy, my youngest cousin. Through the ensuing years we have had countless conversations and it warms my heart she has taken on a task to share a part of "our" history. Ray was my Dad Maynard's middle brother.

Thank you, Elizabeth Grey, for sharing just a snippet of the history of a really unique, wonderful lady, my Aunt Steffi.

-Joy Carlson, September 2022

INTRODUCTION

"Brunch With Steffi" is the result of an impromptu conversation I had with my mother-in-law during her unexpected visit to my home in Libby, Montana. What began as "small talk" ended in a very heavy conversation about her imprisonment and journey to freedom from a German concentration camp. Her journey took place during and immediately after WWII and resulting in her becoming a war bride. As our chat grew more in depth, I could feel my excitement building. I realized she had lived first-hand the horrors of a time in history I had only read about in history books. I took notes franticly to record some of the details significant to her experience. Our chat turned into several hours of dialogue. My mind raced to consider how I could fill in the blanks later by asking other family members and friends to confirm what I had written down. To my utter shock, I discovered years later that Steffi had never revealed some of these details to anyone else!

Through many hours of research and interviews I began to know Steffi in a way that humanized and personalized the holocaust. I consulted with a historian who advised me to humanize her experience. He said extensive data about this time in history had been recorded ad nauseam. The more I investigated, the more I felt burdened with the idea that she had entrusted these facts to me for reasons I would never know. A few years after our discussion, Steffi rapidly developed dementia. Any remaining details were lost to this disease.

I believe the world needs to be constantly reminded of the costliness of sitting on the sidelines and refusing to get involved when we are conscious of crimes. Whether in our own country or on foreign soil, when crimes are being committed against our fellow man, we must intervene. "The only thing necessary for the triumph of evil is for good men to do nothing."

CHAPTER 1

SMALL TALK

During the early years of our marriage, my husband, Randy, and I made several trips each year to Libby, Montana, his hometown. Located in northwest Montana and nestled along the banks of the Kootenai River between the Cabinet Mountain range and the Purcell Mountains, this rural, small town provided a welcomed break from the hustle and bustle of city life. We owned and operated an events center in southern Alabama which meant business hours could be seven days a week and any hours of the day or night. Between the functions at our events business and limo service, we barely had time to get enough sleep, much less take any leisure time for stress relief. These Montana visits included gatherings with friends and family for any outdoor activities we could squeeze into the schedule. The trip we made in 2009 was on track to be just the getaway we needed.

The crisp Montana air was a refreshing change from the thick humid atmosphere of Alabama. This particular trip was during the summer months when Montana has cool evenings and warm days. We were fortunate enough to own an acre lot on the Kootenai River with water, sewer, and electric hook-ups which allowed us to park our motorhome along the bank of the river. We enjoyed most of the modern comforts of home. The pleasant weather allowed for open windows in the morning to enjoy the sounds of the river flowing over the rocks and the music of the birds chirping. If you were an early riser, you could witness bald eagles fishing in the river at sunrise. Our little slice of paradise had a million dollar view.

A couple of days into our trip, Randy decided to take a day and spend it with some of his old high school buddies. I was thrilled at the thought of some alone time without the usual distractions of electronic devices. We had no telephone service or TV connection and cell service was spotty at best. I know, sounds nuts, but it was great!

The scarcity of technology meant that visitors often dropped by unannounced! Actually, we had already contacted everyone we intended to see before getting into town and we probably knew when we could expect a guest. I had not scheduled any time with friends on this day and thought I had most of the day to clear my head or possibly take a long walk on the trail at the end of our road. God obviously had other plans for how I was to spend my time.

About an hour after breakfast, I was finishing up some chores before sitting down to take in my surroundings. In preparation for a mid-morning cup of tea, I had a kettle of water heating on the propane stove. Then I heard a vehicle coming down our gravel driveway. As I pulled back the curtains to investigate, I saw my mother-in-law, Steffi, getting out of her car. My immediate thought was that she probably wouldn't stay very long when she found out that Randy was not with me. Randy and I had only been married a few years and we had lived in Alabama the entire time. Therefore, I had not had the chance to get to know my mother-in-law. The extent of our contact included family gatherings and short conversations over long-distance phone calls. My impression of her was that she was a fine Christian woman who was devoted to her church and family. She had always been cordial to me and she seemed to appreciate when I would play church hymns for her on the piano.

Steffi knocked politely. I opened the door and invited her in for some tea. She graciously accepted. I had prepared muffins and home-made chocolate treats (I prefer chocolate instead of coffee for my caffeine fix). As we began to enjoy a snack, we started with the usual small talk topics of weather, family, and social activities. Weather in Montana as compared to Alabama was an easy conversation starter. Due to former visits to Alabama, Steffi was aware of the humidity levels during the summer months. During an early visit down South, she had met my family even before I developed a relationship with her son. Naturally, she was curious about how my family was doing.

Small talk continued by discussing Steffi's social life. Once a week Steffi played Pinochle with a group of ladies she had known almost since she arrived in Libby. But, her social life centered around her church. She and her husband, Ray, had both been raised Roman Catholic and they served the church faithfully in several capacities. They helped with daily mass, sang in the choir, prepared food for bake sales and attended potluck dinners. All three of her children (Christine, Caran, and Randy) were raised to attend church regularly and observe Christian holidays with reverence. Ray had been a faithful member of the Catholic Knights Of Columbus.

I was curious about how her life in Poland compared to life in the United States. She told me that Libby reminded her a lot of her homeland. The weather and terrain in northwest Montana is similar to that of her native region of Poland. Culturally, she adjusted through her connection with the church. As with most war brides, she was encouraged to speak only English and to abandon her native language of Polish as well as the German she spoke. Years later, her children regretted never asking their mom about her Polish background or ever learning any of the language.

Steffi quizzed me about whether or not I liked the northwest and would be willing to move to the area. I informed her I did like that part of the country and hoped to move there someday. However, our business needed much attention and nurturing before we could think about selling it and relocating. I told her this would probably not happen soon. She indicated she completely understood! Steffi shared with me that she and Ray, Randy's father, had made several attempts at some business ventures. One major flop was owning and operating a gas station. Randy had already told me what a difficult time his dad had collecting from customers for money owed when they ran the gas station!

Looking out the window at sunshine sparkling on the river, Steffi began to talk about the property she and her late husband, Ray, had had

on Bull Lake (a lake 20 miles outside of town.) She
began to reminisce about the good times the
family enjoyed on the weekends while at their
little spot. They had a small camper they left on
their lot and built a dock for their fiberglass sport
boat. The kids swam and water-skied when they
became old enough. Evidently, many happy family
gatherings occurred out on this shoreline which
included the two grandchildren Steven and
Brianna. Her demeanor seemed to be happy upon
recalling these memories. She related how she
still missed Ray 15 years after his massive heart
attack. This prompted me to inquire further about
how their story together began.

Steffi and Ray had a unique love story. Steffi
was from Poland and met Ray when he was
deployed to Germany while in the Army during
WWII. I questioned her about the circumstances
of their romance. At first, she gave me just the
highlights: She worked in the cafeteria of a
hospital where Ray was the cook. After Ray met
her socially at a dinner party, he tried for weeks to

get her to go on a date until she agreed to a double date with another couple. During WWII, young ladies in Europe were often taken advantage of by lonely GI's and later left them with nothing but a broken heart. Steffi reported knowing several girls who found out they were pregnant and then discovered that their Gi boyfriends were married! She was naturally cautious!

In the 1940s, life for women without any male family members to help navigate the pathways of life could be difficult and even dangerous in times of war. Women of my generation and younger find it almost impossible to imagine lacking the freedoms and opportunities that we are afforded today. Left with no other options, these young women, hell-bent on survival, found ways to carve out a life that would benefit later generations. Still, sometimes it seems we take one step backward for every two steps forward when it comes to equality for men and women. Overall, though, things are much better and continue to improve.

By now, my curiosity was almost in peak mode! The natural progression of questioning was wanting to know how she ended up in Germany when she was from Poland. I was not a history buff and could not reason how she, as a Catholic, had been driven from her home. Hadn't the target for the Nazis been the Jews?

CHAPTER 2

IMPRISONED AND ENSLAVED

A family friend told me Steffi had lived in a "work camp" during WWII before she met Ray. My concept of a work camp was far from what the reality turned out to be! Steffi's revelations and the research I conducted revealed how lacking in knowledge most Americans are about the WWII era. These "work camps" were precursors to the concentration/extermination camps. They were sites where slave labor was used to build the torture chambers! To quote George Santayana, "Those who do not remember the past are condemned to repeat it." This is engraved on a wall at the Auschwitz memorial site in Poland.

Steffi is the youngest of three daughters born to Josef Petruch and Kataryna Cogla. She was born on May 24, 1924, in Stry, Stanislawow, Poland (now Lviv, Oblast, Ukraine). Steffi's sisters were actually half-sisters from previous marriages of both parents. The oldest sibling was already married with a child when the war broke out and the middle daughter was perhaps engaged, but still living at home. Josef Petruch was deceased at the time Poland was invaded and the circumstances surrounding his death are unknown.

Stry, Poland, like most of Poland since around 1000 AD, was populated with a significant number of Catholics. It had also been a Jewish settlement area for centuries. This Judeo-Christian community functioned for many years as a productive society boasting machine factories and numerous agriculture endeavors. The Polish people were aware of the discrimination against the Jews in Germany. This had been occurring for many years. In general, Polish culture was tolerant of diversity. It seemed unlikely that German racist policies would infiltrate the Polish government. The Polish people were confident in the ability of their military to protect them from foreign enemies. So, the citizens were shocked when their country was conquered so swiftly! Because Polish citizens were not allowed to bear arms, the Germans and Russians were met with very little resistance.

Steffi was only 15 years old when the war broke out in Poland. On September 1, 1939, Nazi Germany invaded Poland from the west. Then, on September 17, 1939, the Soviet Union invaded Poland from the east. Military operations continued until October 6, 1939, when all of Poland had been conquered. The country was divided between Russia and Germany, per the German-Soviet Nonaggression Pact. This pact, signed on August 23, 1939, outlined how the countries would divide Eastern Europe after they anticipated defeat. Steffi's hometown of Stry, south of Warsaw, was initially given to Russia. Because of the location of her region of Poland, battles between Russia and Germany continued over the exact borderlines. Therefore, she was exposed to both Russian and German tyranny. Even though the Germans were responsible for the mass extermination of Jews and other dissidents, the Russians committed their share of atrocities.

After the conquest, the Nazi's wasted no time initiating the ground work necessary to carry out their "Final Solution" (a plan for the genocide of Jews). They immediately began construction on both "Provisional Concentration Camps" and "Transit Camps". Provisional Concentration Camps were created to detain Poles who had been suspected of organizing Polish civilian resistance against the German invaders. The Transit Camps were for detention of Polish POWs. More than 100,000 Poles were detained. Cruel interrogation of the camp prisoners was followed by mass executions, taking place mostly in the forests nearby.

In addition to these provisional concentration camps, construction on more stationary sites (mostly Jewish property) was begun using land confiscated from citizens. These more permanent structures would eventually become the death camps where gas chambers were used to exterminate the Jews, political dissidents and agitators. Until the May, 1946, completion of the first camp, known as KL Auschwitz I, Jewish citizens were detained in separate areas known as ghettos. After their personal property and rights as citizens were taken away, Jews were often transported to one of the ghettos to be used as slave labor.

Initially, Steffi and her family managed to avoid being involved in any mass reassignment, but Nazi greed eventually prevailed. Perhaps because Steffi and her family lived in one of the predominantly Jewish communities, they were taken to one of the ghettos along with their neighbors. Given the depressed economy and lack of available jobs, Steffi's mom probably depended on assistance from her neighbors, who were mostly Jewish, to maintain her household. Her family may have also known that many of the Catholic priests were executed in an effort to deter dissidents. So, she may have gone willingly into a ghetto hoping to remain connected with her support group.   She and her family had heard the horror stories about the conditions in these encampments. The reality proved to be even worse!

Given it's close proximity to Stry, Tarnow is the most likely location of Steffi's encampment. The living conditions described by Steffi align with all other descriptions most of us have heard and seen on the television documentaries, or read about in the many books written on the subject. The lack of proper sanitation and shortage of food made for some gruesome situations. Steffi rarely shared such details with her family.

The living arrangements in the camp eventually became unbearable. Sanitation was poor and her mother struggled to provide even basics like food and clothing for her two young teenage daughters. Most of the people lived off the generosity of those who could somehow acquire extra rations. Steffi has memories of neighbors frequently knocking on the family's door begging for any extra food that could be spared. She vividly described how she watched a man die of starvation on the steps of her house! He was so emaciated that his ribs could be seen and he could hardly walk. Unfortunately, this was a common scene that played out daily in the streets of the ghettos.

To make matters worse, random harassment from government officials made simply walking down the street a possible crime. One day Steffi was with a group of friends in town when a law enforcement officer approached the teens. He interrogated them with intimidating questions about where they were going and for what purpose. For unknown reasons, Steffi was taken into custody. When she arrived at the police station, the officers conducted a lengthy interview with Steffi about her family. She was released without charges. However, a short time later she and her family were herded onto a train car with other residents headed for another slave labor camp (believed to be Ravensbruck, the largest Nazi camp for women located north of Berlin).

The train transport to Ravensbruck is believed to have been sometime in the fall of 1940. Steffi and her family never made it to Germany. During transit, the train was bombed by the Russians and everyone on board scattered. Steffi was separated from her family in the chaos. She was captured and sent to a c KL Auschwitz I until she was transferred to Auschwitz II Birkenau sometime after August, 1942. Female prisoners were relocated to Auschwitz II then bused to the various work locations where their slave labor was needed. She was part of the general slave labor pool with special language skills. Her ability to speak several languages made her useful as an interpreter when information was needed from prisoners. As long as prisoners were physically able to perform their duties, they were often treated relatively humanely. According to Steffi, whether Germans or Russians were in control, cruelty was directed at anyone who did not comply with their ideals.

The camps were constructed in sections to enclose different complexes making them independent of one another. Inmates in the internal complex were allowed to eat, sleep, and work in these compounds. External complexes consisted of gas chambers and cremation furnaces. Incoming transportees went either to the slave labor internal complex or directly by railcar to the external complex for execution. Because the women were known to have endured more extreme torture than the men in these camps, one can only imagine the atrocities Steffi witnessed! She did not share any of these details with me, but she did relay how difficult it was to mentally deal with knowing what was happening to her fellow humans.

At the labor camps, death and mistreatment were everywhere. The people who could not live through the ordeal of torture and starvation as well as those who were executed in the gas chambers, were buried in mass graves on the edges of the compound. According to historians, the genocide was occurring at such a rapid rate that it was not unusual for the guards to create mass graves overnight. Therefore, making it possible to walk over the graves and be unaware of what was buried under your feet! Steffi described her experience with one of these sites as feeling as if an earthquake were occurring. At the time of our conversation, I was unaware of these details about the camps and did not understand the gruesome scene Steffi was trying to recount. Thinking back on the conversation, I'm not sure she realized what she was experiencing at that moment. (Whether she felt people who were buried alive trying to get out or the gas created by decomposing bodies is unclear. However, she did seem genuinely unnerved by this memory, so I did not ask any further questions to get details.)

As a form of psychological torture, the inmates were cut off from the outside world with no form of communication. The only way to get information about the outside world was to speak to new arrivals. Starved for information about their families, the inmates would attempt to talk through the barbed wire fencing to others confined in different barracks. Each block of barracks was enclosed with its own border fence as well as an outer fence defining each sector. This concept allowed the guards to move from one block to another within a protective fencing. This set-up made it easier to keep prisoners under surveillance. The entire compound had an outer fence for added security.

Even with all the security measures, some people managed to escape the camp. Usually, they were captured and returned to be tortured and humiliated in front of the other prisoners as a deterrent to those who might be considering the same action. The guards were ruthless to anyone they perceived as a threat to their authority.

One of the ways the guards kept track of inmate ethnicity and/or political affiliation was to make them wear color stripes on their uniforms. Polish political prisoners were marked with a red triangle on their clothing. Because of this humiliation, Steffi refused to wear red for the rest of her life!

Rumors of regime change often circulated among the inmates, but regardless of who was in charge, not much changed for the prisoners. The daily grind of hard labor in industrial factories remained constant. Jews and political prisoners continued to be murdered at increasing rates. It seemed their nightmare would never end! Then, one day in January, 1945, Steffi and the others woke up to a deserted camp. Could they finally be free from their captors?

The guards had left so abruptly that remaining prisoners looked around in disbelief at the deserted camp. They knew a decision had to be made quickly about whether to stay or flee. If they stayed, then they risked the Germans returning to continue the genocide. Or, perhaps, the Russians might arrive soon to seize the area. Neither of these choices were pleasant to consider. (Even though the Russians were not committing mass genocide, Steffi had witnessed first-hand how badly the Russians treated Polish citizens. While the Nazis were concerned with race and religion, the Russians judged prisoners by social status.) A third possibility was that the Allied Forces might come to their rescue. Not being sure of the correct scenario, all able-bodied prisoners scattered into the country to hide. Steffi and two other women teamed up to increase their odds for survival. Unfortunately, most prisoners were in such poor health or physical condition that they were unable to flee. These are the emaciated creatures that the Russian Red Army discovered when they reached the camp on January 27, 1945.

CHAPTER 3

JOURNEY TO FREEDOM

Steffi and the two other women who decided to stay together after leaving the concentration camp navigated the countryside almost exclusively at night. Getting past the soldiers and guards was easier under the cover of darkness. Even though the Russians had liberated their camp, a fluid situation made it difficult to determine boundary lines. Control of certain areas was constantly changing. Germany had controlled Poland since June, 1941, and maintained the territory until January, 1945. Then the Russians retaliated due to Germany breaking the Nonaggression Pact.

Both German and Russian soldiers were hostile to Polish citizens. Poles were considered the conquered people. When the circumstances required the ladies to cross through an official checkpoint, Steffi did most of the talking due to her excellent language skills. She often was able to disguise their nationality and/or area of origin.

During daylight hours, the women would hide in ditches or abandoned buildings, keeping watch for any activity and possible clues as to the status of the war. Supply sources were scarce and they had to resort to stealing food in order to survive. Occasionally, a kind citizen would give them assistance with food and shelter. Accepting help from strangers was dangerous because it was hard to discern who might be a Nazi sympathizer. The pressure on ordinary citizens to report about their neighbors was extreme.   Often, deadly consequences resulted if someone was discovered assisting dissidents such as Steffi's group. At any moment, a wrong decision could send them back to the hell hole from which they had escaped!

The fear and adversity these young ladies had to overcome to make this journey with no money, no supplies, and no support was incredible. Their determination and resolve took them forward against seemingly insurmountable odds! As I listened to Steffi recount some of the details of this time in her life, I wondered if the generations of women following her could have survived the tumultuous times she endured. Our world has become pampered with instant gratification when it comes to both services and manufactured goods. What would she think of the current unrest in our society rooted in complaints of hurt feelings and perceived unfairness. The freedoms that her husband, Ray, fought to defend are currently being questioned as white supremacy. The Nazi white supremacy discrimination policies and acts of cruelty against their fellow human beings was rooted in decades of perceived injustice from one category of citizens towards another. These crimes against humanity have been glossed over and diminished in some of our history lessons. We should remember every story that has been told and remind ourselves that "The only thing necessary for the triumph of evil is for good men to do nothing." Thankfully, the Allied Forces, encouraged by Winston Churchill, found it necessary to act when the oppressed could not act for themselves.

The journey to freedom for Steffi and her friends took months to complete. Sometime in the spring or early summer of 1945, the ladies arrived at a hospital in Regensburg, Germany. Tired, hungry, and in poor health, they were given the necessary health care and provided with nutrition to regain their strength. They found employment in some of the local industries.   Steffi established residency in Regensburg on August 16, 1945, after getting work at the 250th Station Hospital established by the US Army on June 14, 1945. The area hospitals were operated by Catholic organizations before the US arrived to take over. This could explain Steffi's decision to find safety and security at this facility.   Ray was stationed with this medical unit as one of the cooks in the Army. Steffi worked in the food service area distributing trays to patients as well as performing other food service tasks.

Throughout her first months in Regensburg, I would imagine Steffi was desperately trying to settle into a new home and get into a routine to establish some form of normalcy in her life. Adjusting to the fact that she might never see her family again was a mental battle she fought while trying to avoid being swept off her feet by a military boy. She was thankful to have escaped the hell of the past few years. A heartbreak was not something she wanted to add to her psychological burden. Then, along came Ray Carlson.

Ray was persistent in his pursuit of Steffi. He desperately tried to prove his intentions were honorable. Over the next several months, Steffi began to warm up to Ray's outgoing personality. Eventually, Steffi became convinced that Ray was trustworthy and she dated him regularly for almost a year. Ray proposed marriage and they were married in Regensburg on Friday, February 14, 1947. A reception in their honor was held the following day at the Men's Club of the Station Hospital. They shared the celebration with another couple who had been married earlier that day.

Having found the love of her life, Steffi was still haunted by the mystery of what had happened to her family. One of the ladies who accompanied her on her journey to freedom began planning to return to the Polish territory to find her family. Steffi felt the situation was still too unstable to return, but her friend insisted on going. Steffi took her to the train station and wished her luck. Fortunately, Steffi's friend returned to Regensberg unharmed, but the friend's report on matters back in Poland was not encouraging. This friend had managed to make it into the region where she believed her family might be located. However, she was constantly followed and interrogated by government officials. She felt an arrest was inevitable. So, she returned without any helpful information.

As the war ended and Ray approached the possible end to his deployment, the couple initiated procedures for Steffi to join Ray when he left for the United States. The effort to bring home the thousands of servicemen from abroad was a daunting task. Many of the GI's had gotten married or engaged while overseas. The immigration process was tedious due to the

Immigration Act of 1924. This act restricted the numbers of immigrants from each country who could enter America. Fortunately, the United States government had enacted legislation known as the "War Brides Act of 1945." This bill allowed the spouses who were not citizens of the United States (as well as children of military personnel born abroad) to come to the United States without all the red tape usually accompanying the process.

As they waited for government approval, Steffi became pregnant with their first child. Their daughter, Christine, was born in Regensburg, Germany, before they returned to the United States. Negotiating the transport of a mother and a child was more challenging than an individual trip, but, they got through it and Steffi joined Ray on the ship home.

On the journey to the United States, Steffi spent most of her time in sick bay due to being sea sick. (She never wanted to go boating after her cruise across the Atlantic! After they bought a waterfront lot on Bull Lake, Ray and the kids enjoyed water sports while Steffi often watched from the shoreline.) Since the servicemen were kept in separate rooms from passengers, even when married, Ray had to come get the baby during the day so Steffi could try to rest. As a result, Steffi lost several pounds during the two-week trip.

CHAPTER 4

A WAR BRIDE IN AMERICA

After disembarking onto American soil in New York City, New York, on July 29, 1948, Ray and Steffi began to make their way across the United States towards Montana, stopping in Pennsylvania to visit friends who had served in Germany with Ray. Steffi was even featured in the Brownsville Telegraph in the Brownsville, Pennsylvania, local newspaper as a concentration camp survivor. Ray's parents (Fred and Delina Carlson) and grandparents (Mr. and Mrs. Roy) drove to Brownsville, Pennsylvania, to meet Ray, Steffi, and Christine (their eighth-month-old toddler born in Regensburg, Germany). Ray's parents and grandparents accompanied them back to Libby, Montana.

Once they reached Libby, Montana, Steffi became one of only 100 war brides who settled in Montana after WWII. In the town of Libby, only one other war bride is known to have established residence. The adjustment period for a war bride was often made more difficult by the pressure to abandon her native language and speak only

English. To Steffi, speaking only English was a minor concession considering her experiences so far! She concentrated on being a faithful wife and loving mother.

Ray and Steffi soon welcomed their second child, Caran, born in Libby on May 5, 1949. While they were living in a log home on the edge of town, Ray bought a gas station that proved to be financially unstable. During these economically challenging times, Steffi decided she needed to get a job and contribute to the household budget. Her first job in Libby was at the Caboose Motel where she worked in the restaurant as a waitress. She began her long career at Hafferman's Thrift Grocery Store in the small diner associated with the store as a short order cook. Randy remembers stopping by after school for a burger and a coke float. Eventually, she transferred to the meat department as a meat wrapper where she worked until she retired.

A few years later, Ray retired a few years after Steffi from W. R. Grace after working over 25 years in their Zonolite mine just outside of Libby, Montana. Spending time with the kids and grandkids filled most of their time as well as camping, playing cards, and traveling with friends. They were able to enjoy 10 years of retirement together before Ray died suddenly of a heart attack. (Unfortunately, Ray was one of the employees who developed heart issues as a result of his exposure to the dust created during the mining process. Actually, Steffi, Randy, and Christine developed Asbestosis from their exposure to the dust via his clothes when he came home from work.)

Assimilation for Steffi came without a lot of complications. However, she still suffered heartache and sorrow in some of the same ways most of us do throughout our lives. One of the most devastating was probably the near fatal car crash of her daughter, Christine. Gestational diabetes is believed to have played a key role in causing Christine to fall asleep at the wheel while experiencing a hypoglycemic episode. The car veered off the road and hit a mailbox post that came through the windshield. The post hit her in the right eye. At the time, Christine was 23 years old and pregnant with her son. She remained in critical condition for a long time and underwent multiple surgeries to repair the extensive damage to her face and back. She suffered several meningitis infections that resulted in permanent hemiparesis on the right side of her body. She lost her right eye and used a leg brace and walker for ambulation. The main miracle from this ordeal was that her son was born healthy and unharmed.

Steffi never really came to terms with Christine's disabilities. I think Steffi had overcome such obstacles when she was Christine's age that when her daughter seemed to give up on her therapy sessions, Steffi could not be sympathetic. Christine's husband was not emotionally able to handle the situation and divorced her shortly after she returned home from her last hospital stay. As a result, Ray became the main caregiver. He made many attempts to encourage Christine to find ways to spend her time productively with hobbies like knitting and crocheting. Ray and Steffi transported Christine and her hand-made items to countless festivals. Their hope was to make her feel like a productive member of society as well as to increase her self-esteem. At the time of the accident, Christine had a promising career with the Corp of Engineers at the Libby Dam in the administrative office. In today's world, she could probably have returned to this job with reasonable accommodations for her acquired disability.

Steffi and Ray had a second child shortly after coming to the United States from Germany. They welcomed another daughter, Caran, in May of 1949. Caran married a hometown boy who joined the Army. When Caran joined her husband in Germany for an accompanied tour, Ray and Steffi began to plan a visit.

Even though Steffi had her green card for many years, she did not take the United States citizenship test until June, 1979. The thought of the testing intimidated her. She was fearful of failing the test and being sent back to Poland. However, Steffi overcame her fear and became a citizen of the United States in order to travel abroad to visit her daughter. Steffi wanted to have an American passport when she traveled abroad because she felt being an American citizen would protect her from being detained anywhere in the world. She had been separated from her birth family and could not comprehend living through the nightmare of being torn away from more loved ones!

Ray and Steffi visited Caran in Regensburg, Germany. Among the activities was a return to the church where they were married. During this trip, Steffi might have enjoyed seeing some of her long-lost family members in nearby Poland, but she was still leery of returning to her home country. Steffi had received a certified letter from an uncle back in the early 70s which she refused to accept. Randy was home when the letter came and he could not understand why his mother did not want to acknowledge the correspondence. When Ray got home from work later that day, Randy mentioned the incident to his dad. After Ray discussed it with Steffi, Randy was told never to speak of the letter again. The only explanation given to Randy was that Steffi did not want to associate with this relative in any way. (We assume he was a Nazi sympathizer.)

Until Steffi's death on October 24, 2014, no one could understand how her uncle was able to locate her in America. What none of the family ever knew was that Steffi had had previous contact with one of her sisters. While sorting through letters and official documents after her death, they found a letter written in what appeared to be Polish and dated in late 1956. An acquaintance of mine from Poland interpreted the letter and we discovered it was from her sister.

The letter was a combination of Polish and Ukrainian languages making it difficult to determine some of the exact wording. It seemed to be more of a letter to enquire about Steffi's husband and kids than the type of correspondence you might have with a family member, especially a sister. The person identified herself as her sister, Anna Domendiak, and gave the names of her children. She asked if Steffi was happy and healthy. She also asked Steffi to write a response to her letter. The interpreter mentioned that the way she addressed Steffi was as more of a casual acquaintance than a family member. We assume that Steffi's uncle was able to locate Steffi through this sister. If Steffi had attempted to communicate with her sister, we could not find any evidence or documentation to support it. We believe that after receiving the letter from her uncle, Steffi was too afraid to make any further contact with family in Poland.

I think the letter from her long-lost uncle was one of the main reasons Steffi refused to travel outside the United States until she became an American citizen. She believed deep down that the monsters responsible for her holocaust experience would hunt down everyone who knew anything about their demonic behavior and eliminate the threat. These fears might have seemed baseless. However, during the last few decades, we have come to realize that the communist regime sends operatives into every country to execute former members as well as their families in an effort to discourage future asylum seekers. Obviously, Steffi's psychological scars never healed. In fact, during the last few months of her life, when her cognition was functioning at a minimal level, she would speak almost exclusively in Polish and scream out in horror at night. One can only imagine the nightmares that haunted her memory.

FINAL THOUGHTS

By all accounts, Steffi embraced her new homeland as well as her new family with thankfulness. Ray had two brothers who lived in Montana, along with their wives and children. They stayed in touch with Steffi giving her some added family connections. Churches have always provided a great source for families to get connected with their communities and make friends with similar interests. As mentioned earlier, Steffi remained a loyal member of the Catholic church in Libby, Saint Joseph's Catholic Church.

Steffi's story is not unique in her circumstances. It is inspiring because of the outcome. She managed to carve out a stable family life for herself and her children despite her psychological scars from the past. By withholding the gruesome details of her ordeal in Poland, she built relationships based on her character and not out of some sense of obligation or sympathy for her. She was able to grow into the person she wanted to be and not let her past define her.

I became compelled to write books about people who have overcome adversity after going through a painful divorce. I remember the feeling of being alone in my emotional trauma when my mother began to send me inspirational books to read. At first, I read them out of respect for my mother's attempt to help me deal with my heartache. But, as I read, I found myself feeling less alone and more confident to move on in life. The individuals who were willing to share their walk through the dark valleys of life became my motivation to persevere.

My first book was about my childhood survival from a severe burn and how it shaped my life both personally and professionally. After I sent the book to family and friends, I received encouraging reviews from them. It was interesting to hear how many different perspectives came out of the same book. As a result, I was inspired to tell the stories of others who have overcome adversity. My hope is that Steffi's triumphant story will bring comfort to others who might have suffered similar horrific events in their lives and provide some enlightening words to get them through whatever trials and tribulations they may be facing.

ABOUT THE AUTHOR

Elizabeth Grey was born and raised in the southern United States. She currently lives in the northwest United States. Elizabeth enjoys listening to the personal history of her friends and family. Her books are about people who have survived tragic events in their lives and persevered to become productive individuals. During a painful period in her life, Elizabeth found inspirational books by others who had experienced similar heartache to be very helpful to her. She endeavors to bring that same sense of encouragement to her readers.

Please visit http://ElizabethGrey.pubsitepro.com to learn more about her and the history behind her books.

www.ingramcontent.com/pod-product-compliance
Lightning Source LLC
Chambersburg PA
CBHW041402160426
42812CB00090B/2626